ATHLETICS

Andy Croft

Published in association with The Basic Skills Agency

Hodder & Stoughton

A MEMBER

Acknowledgements

Cover: Getty Images

Photos: p. 2 © Glyn Kirk/Action Plus; p. 6 © Michael Steele/Getty Images; pp. 11, 27 © Tony Duffy/Allsport; pp. 15, 24 © Tony Marshall/EMPICS; p. 19 © Don Morley/EMPICS.

Every effort has been made to trace copyright holders of material reproduced in this book. Any rights not acknowledged will be acknowledged in subsequent printings if notice is given to the publisher.

Basic Skills
Collection

Orders; please contact Bookpoint Ltd, 130 Milton Park, Abingdon, Oxon OX14 4SB. Telephone (44) 01235 827720, Fax: (44) 01235 400454. Lines are open from 9.00–6.00, Monday to Saturday, with a 24 hour message answering service. You can also order through our website www.hodderheadline.co.uk

British Library Cataloguing in Publication Data
A catalogue record for this title is available from the British Library

ISBN 0 340 87308 6

First published 2003
Impression number   10 9 8 7 6 5 4 3 2 1
Year   2007 2206 2005 2004 2003

Typeset by SX Composing DTP, Rayleigh, Essex.
Printed in Great Britain for Hodder & Stoughton Educational, a division of Hodder Headline, 338 Euston Road, London NW1 3BH by The Bath Press Ltd, Bath.

Contents

1 Beginnings

People have always enjoyed
running, jumping and throwing.

Over 3000 years ago, in Greece,
the best athletes competed against each other.
They met every four years
at a place called Olympus.
This was called the Olympic Games.

They organised running races,
chariot races, boxing and wrestling.
They invented the long jump,
the discus, javelin, shot put
and pentathlon.
They even ran races wearing armour.

Winners on the podium.

The winners of the Greek games
didn't win money or medals.
They were given flowers and poems!

Today the best athletes in the world
still compete against each other
every four years.
It is still called the Olympic Games.

The first modern Olympics were held in 1896.
Only men were allowed to enter.
In 1900, women joined in for the first time.
They were only allowed to enter three events:
tennis, golf and yachting.

2 Running

100 metres

The shortest race is the 100 metres sprint.

It is also the fastest.

You have to be fast to run 100 metres.

Very fast.

Olympic runners are so fast,

they hold their breath all the way.

Sprinters used to start from a standing position,

but now they use starting blocks.

Cecil Lee set the first modern record in 1892.

He ran 100 yards in 10.8 seconds.

Tim Montgomery set a new world record in 2002.

He ran 100 metres in 9.78 seconds –

only one second faster!

Florence Griffith-Joyner

is the fastest ever woman.

She ran 100 metres in 10.49 seconds.

200 metres

To run 200 metres,
you have to be as fast
as a 100-metre sprinter.
You also need good balance
to run round the bend in the track.

400 metres

The 400 metre race is a killer.
If you run at top speed for more than 35 seconds,
your legs start hurting.
400-metre runners must be fast.
You must be able to run round bends.
You must be able to pace yourself.
And you must learn to ignore pain!

Michelle Ballentine of Jamaica in action.

800 metres

The first 300 metres are run in lanes.
Then you are allowed to swap lanes.
You need speed, endurance,
balance and good tactics.
Do you run from the front and force the pace?
Do you wait till the last lap
and then try to take the lead?
What do you do if you are 'boxed in'
behind other runners?

1500 metres

This is just under a mile.
In 1954 Roger Bannister became the first person
to run a mile in less than four minutes.
The best 1500-metre runners today
are from North Africa.

Steeplechase

The steeplechase began as a bet
between Oxford students in 1850.
They wanted to see if athletes
could run like horses.
You have to run round a 400-metre track,
jumping over hurdles and a high water jump.
The steeplechase distance is usually
2000 metres or 3000 metres.
Runners from Kenya have won
every Olympic steeplechase since 1984.

Hurdles

Hurdlers have to be fast.
They have to be good at jumping.
They have to run and jump at the same time.
The world record holder is Kevin Young.
He is nicknamed 'Spiderman'.
His legs are so long,
he only takes twelve steps between each hurdle.

Long Distance Running

2,500 years ago a Greek soldier
ran 40 kilometres
from Marathon to Athens.
The longest running race
is still called the Marathon.

At the 1908 London Olympics,
athletes ran from Windsor Castle
to the White City stadium.
Then they had to run two-thirds
of a lap on the track,
just so they finished in front of the royal box.
The distance was 42,195 metres
(just over 26 miles).
This became the official Marathon distance.

At the 1904 Olympic Games in St Louis
one Marathon runner had a lift in a car!
In 1960, the Olympic gold medal was won
by a runner who did not wear any shoes!

3 Jumping

High Jump

High jumpers are usually tall and thin.

You are allowed three jumps at each height.

You can't take off with both feet.

High jumpers used to land feet first.

Today, top high jumpers jump

over the bar backwards and land on a mattress.

This is called the Fosbury Flop.

Other ways of jumping are

the Scissor Jump

and the Western Roll.

Long Jump

About 3,000 years ago,

Greek athletes used to carry stones in each hand.

This helped them to jump further.

The longest jump ever is 8.95 metres.

Dick Fosbury doing the Fosbury Flop.

Triple Jump

The Greeks used to do
three long jumps after another.
Today the triple jump is a hop, a step and a jump.
In 1995, Britain's Jonathan Edwards
became the first triple jumper
to jump more than 60 feet (18.29 metres).

Pole Vault

The Greeks used long poles to jump over bulls.
To be a good pole vaulter,
you need the speed of a sprinter
and the balance of a gymnast.
You run as fast as you can
towards the bar.
Then you push the pole
into the 'box' on the floor.

Athletes used to climb up the pole in midair.
Today they swing upside down
when the pole begins to bend.
The world record pole vault
is 6.15 metres.

4 Throwing

Javelin

Hercules was one of
the earliest javelin throwers.
The Greeks used to throw spears at a target.
To throw the javelin, you have to be fast.
You also have to be strong.
You run as fast as you can
and throw the javelin as far as possible.
The world record javelin throw is 98 metres.

Discus

The discus is like a metal Frisbee.
The Greeks used to throw discs
made out of stone or bronze.
They weighed 6 kilograms.
Today the discus weighs 1 kilogram.
You stand in a throwing circle.
You can't step outside this.
Then you spin round and round very fast
and let go of the discus.
The world record discus throw is 74.08 metres.

Shelley Drew of Great Britain.

Shot Put

Hundreds of years ago
soldiers had cannonball-throwing competitions.
The shot is like a cannonball.
It weighs 7 kilograms.
Shot putters need strength and balance.
You stand facing backwards in a throwing circle,
with the shot under your chin.
Then you turn round,
throwing the shot as far away as you can.
You can't step outside the circle.
It is very hard not to bend your arms.
The world record shot put is 23.12 metres.

5 Everything

Some athletes are good at everything.
There are two special competitions
for these special athletes.

The Heptathlon

This event is for top women athletes.
You have to compete in seven events.
It used to be called the pentathlon (five events).
On the first day, you have to
run 200 metres and 100 metre hurdles,
do the shot put and high jump.
On the second day, you have to
do the long jump, throw the javelin
and run 800 metres.

Mary Peters won the Olympic pentathlon
in 1972 with a world record score.
She was 33 years old.
That's pretty old for a top athlete.

The Decathlon

You have to compete
in ten different events in two days.
On the first day, you have to
run 100 metres and 400 metres,
do the long jump, shot put and high jump.
On the second day, you have to
run 110 metre hurdles,
throw the discus and javelin,
pole vault, and run 1500 metres.

You are given points for each event.
The winner is the athlete with the most points.

Athletes who can do all this
must be very tough.
They must be very fit.
They must be all-round athletes.
They must be the greatest athletes in the world!

Daley Thompson won twelve decathlons between 1980–86.

6 Disabled Athletes

Since 1960, the Olympic Games
has included disabled athletes.
Since 1976, the Winter Olympics
have included events for disabled athletes.
These games are called the Paralympics.

Disabled athletes have to be extra tough.
They compete in all the usual events,
plus a few extra.
Like wheelchair basketball
and wheelchair tennis.
There is even wheelchair rugby!

At the Sydney Paralympics in 2000,
there were 4,000 disabled athletes
from 125 countries.
British athletes won 41 gold medals,
43 silver medals and 47 bronze medals.

Britain's Anthony Peddle
is ranked first in the men's powerlifting event.
At the Sydney Paralympics
he lifted 168 kilograms.
That's three and a half times his own weight!

Jason Wening doesn't have any legs.
But he has won three Paralympic gold medals
swimming in the 400 metres freestyle.

Britain's Tanni Grey-Thompson
is the fastest wheelchair racer in the world.
She has won the London Wheelchair Marathon
four times.
She won four gold medals at the Sydney Paralympics:
for the 100 metres, 200 metres,
400 metres and 800 metres races.

There are also special competitions all over the world
for deaf athletes and blind athletes.

Blind athletes are good at lots of sports,
including running, judo, golf and swimming.
They even play cricket and football
with special balls that make a noise when they move.

7 Champions

The greatest athlete of modern times
was Jesse Owens.
He won four gold medals
at the 1936 Olympics:
in the 100 metres,
the 200 metres,
the 400 metres relay
and the long jump.
His 100 metre record
stood for twenty years.
His long jump record
stood for 25 years.
He once set six world records on one day!

Fanny Blankers-Koen made Olympic history
when she won four gold medals
at the 1948 Olympics.
These were for the 100 metres,
200 metres, 80 metre hurdles
and the 100 metres relay.
She also set eight world records.

Michael Johnson was the first man
to win double gold.
He won both the 200 metres and 400 metres
at the 1996 Olympics.

Merlene Ottey has won
seven Olympic medals for sprinting.

Michael Johnson at the 1996 Atlanta Olympic Games.

Haile Gebrselassie
has won four World titles
and two Olympic gold medals in the 10,000 metres.
He is also a world record breaker
at 5,000 metres and 10,000 metres.

Jackie Joyner-Kersee has won
four World and Olympic titles.
She has also won three gold medals
at the long jump.

Javier Sotomayor from Cuba
is the only high jumper who has jumped
over 8 feet (2.45 metres).
That is higher than a football crossbar!

8　Some British All-Time Greats

Britain is only a small country
but it has produced some of the world's best athletes.

Brirain's all-time great include:

Daley Thompson
who won twelve decathlons and a World title.

Sally Gunnell
the only woman to hold the World, European,
Commonwealth and Olympic titles
for the 400 metre hurdles – at the same time.

Linford Christie
who won three World titles for the 100 metres.

Denise Lewis
who won an Olympic gold medal and
three Commonwealth gold medals for
the pentathlon.

Florence Griffith-Joyner (USA) displays her Olympic medals.

9 Some Current World Record Holders

Men's 100 metres

Tim Montgomery, 9.78 seconds (2002)

Women's 100 metres

Florence Griffith-Joyner, 10.49 seconds (1988)

Men's 400 metres

Michael Johnson, 43.18 seconds (1996)

Men's 110 metre hurdles

Colin Jackson, 12.91 seconds (1993)

Women's Marathon

Paula Radcliffe, 2 hours 17 minutes (2002)

Men's Triple Jump

Jonathan Edwards, 18.29 metres (1995)